PORTRAIT OF
TYNESIDE

JASON FRIEND

HALSGROVE

First published in Great Britain in 2009

Title page photograph: *The Swirle Pavilion located along the regenerated Newcastle upon Tyne quayside.*

Prints are available of all of the images in this book via www.jasonfriend.co.uk/tyneside
Images can be licensed for commercial use at www.jasonfriend.co.uk

British Library Cataloguing-in-Publication Data
A CIP record for this title is available from the British Library

ISBN 978 1 84114 886 1

Halsgrove
Halsgrove House,
Ryelands Industrial Estate,
Bagley Road, Wellington, Somerset TA21 9PZ
Tel: 01823 653777 Fax: 01823 216796
email: sales@halsgrove.com

Part of the Halsgrove group of companies
Information on all Halsgrove titles is available at: www.halsgrove.com

Printed and bound by Grafiche Flaminia, Italy

INTRODUCTION

Tyneside is a region where the past, present and future combine to form an eclectic melting pot in the North East of England. Host to the City of Newcastle Upon Tyne and the spiritual home of 'The Geordies', a name derived from the Tyneside miners' use of the George Stevenson safety lamp whilst working down the pits, there is an undeniably strong industrial heritage to be found in the area. History has helped to fuel the common misconception that the area has been shaped upon the industries of a bygone age, and that mankind has been in control of the area's destiny from the very beginning of human settlement.

Of course any resident, Geordie or not, would probably raise a dry smile at this statement. Situated between the Northumberland and Durham Heritage Coasts, the coastline adjoining the North Sea and Tyneside is undoubtedly beautiful, and whilst there are some stretches of the coast that display the marvels of human endeavour to tame nature there are plenty of other stretches that embrace the power of the wild and maintain their natural appearance.

Unquestionably, the heart of Tyneside is the River Tyne, the main artery running from the coast dividing the regions of north and south Tyneside on a journey through Newcastle and beyond. Life on the Tyne has changed throughout the years. The Romans exploited the strategic values of the river by choosing to start the spectacular Hadrian's Wall alongside the Tyne, along with a number of forts that can still be found in Tyneside.

Considering the natural wealth of sea food to be found in the Tyne and the nearby North Sea, it is of little surprise that mankind has been foraging along the Tyne from the earliest days of the period of Roman occupation until modern times. There is still a thriving fishing industry in Tyneside, perhaps best appreciated by an early morning trip to the Fish Quay Market in North Shields.

Recently the face of the Tyne has had a facelift in the form of an ongoing redevelopment plan that has seen a number of luxury apartments, modern architecture and world-class tourist attractions adorn the river. Inland Tyneside is host to a plethora of landscapes including picturesque villages, working agricultural land and sites of historical importance.

A visit to Tyneside has something to offer everyone, whilst for the resident there is always plenty more to discover. Although tourism continues to further increase visitor numbers to the region, many only visit the city or the coast. Perhaps the real Tyneside is a closely guarded Geordie secret. Fortunately they are more than happy to share this secret with the visitor.

ACKNOWLEDGEMENTS

I cannot take all of the credit for the production of this book so I would like to acknowledge the following people who have helped out behind the scenes in one form or another.

Thank you to everyone who I have met whilst working on this book. An extra special thank you to everyone at the St Paul's Monastery and church in Jarrow for their welcoming smiles and the cup of coffee on a cold winter's morning and the Natural History Society of Northumbria for allowing me access to the delightful Gosforth Park Nature Reserve. I am extremely grateful to Roger Holfert of R & K Photographic for the scanning of a selection of the panoramic images and Steven Pugsley and the rest of the team at Halsgrove for making this book a reality.

The support of family and friends is an important ingredient when working on a book of any size so I would like to wholeheartedly thank all of you including John Friend, Penny, Roy and Mark Whitehouse, Valerie Hodgkins, Wayne Hackeson, Steve Hawthorne and Jason Haynes.

As ever my wife, Lynette, has been there to support and encourage me whenever I have most needed it. Thank you for all of your help and unconditional support.

Panoramic view of the River Tyne and Tyne Bridge with the Swing Bridge in the foreground.

Gatehouse of the Tynemouth Castle and Priory, viewed from the west.

East end of the Tynemouth Priory Church, located upon the headland between the River Tyne and the North Sea.

Named Heaton Mill in 1848 although
originally a water corn mill called
Mabel's Mill since 1739, this structure
is now simply known as 'The Mill'.

Tussock on the Town Moor, a large area of common land located within the City of Newcastle Upon Tyne.

The world famous Tyne Bridge spanning the River Tyne in the City of Newcastle Upon Tyne.

Opposite: *Boats moored on the River Tyne with a complex of new apartments located on the North Shields Quayside in the distance.*

Horse grazing in a field located near the former Boldon Colliery in South Tyneside.

Opposite: Abandoned buildings from a bygone age – East Holywell Colliery near Backworth.

The coastline north of St Mary's Island viewed at low tide, looking towards Blyth and the Northumberland border.

Opposite: *The North Sea engulfs the rocky shoreline of Marsden Bay. The sculptured form of the Marsden Rock is testament to the powerful natural forces of this often unrelenting stretch of coast.*

Mist lingers on the River Tyne near Newburn.

Opposite: *A royal-protected swan reflected on a small lake in the Watergate Forest Park.*

View looking from the Armstrong Bridge towards Jesmond Dene.

The golden autumnal colours of the Chopwell Woodland Park managed by the Forestry Commission.

Detail of boats moored on the River Tyne.

Newcastle Quayside and moored river cruise boats, reflected in the still waters of the Tyne.

Train truck used to transport iron ore through what is now Forestry Commission woodland between High Spen and Rowlands Gill.

Opposite: *Details of a steam engine in need of restoration at the Stephenson Railway Museum in West Chirton.*

Nuns Moor with the high-rise flats of Kenton in the distance.

Deciduous canopy in Holywell Dene, a popular pocket of woodland near the Northumberland/Tyneside border.

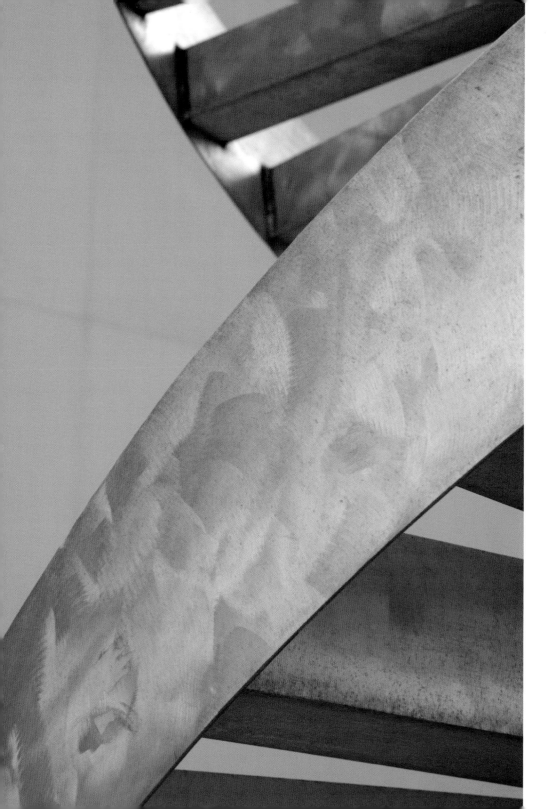

Abstract view of a DNA spiral outside the International Centre for Life in Newcastle Upon Tyne.

Opposite: *The Swan Hunter shipyard near Wallsend.*

The contrasting colours of seaweed against rocks on the North Tyneside coast.

Opposite above: *Arctic Terns hunting for food on the Whitley Bay beach.*

Opposite below: *A collection of seashells, photographed near to St Mary's Island.*

Tom Collins House forms part of the Byker Wall, an award-winning design comprising of a continuous block of maisonettes conceived by Ralph Erskine. In 2007 the wall became a Grade II listed building of outstanding architecture.

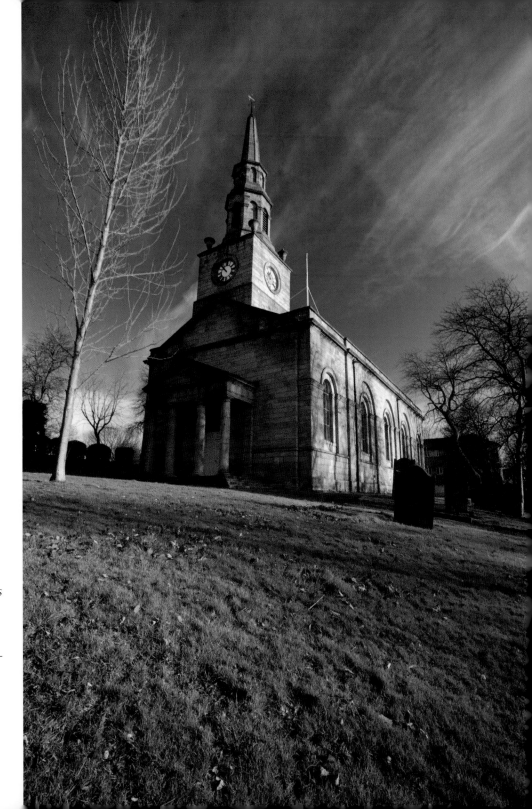

St Ann's Church was originally set in fields overlooking the East Quayside. The church became famous for the distribution of hot soup to the unemployed during the winters of 1908 – 1910 by the vicar, Bernard East.

Farm track running through a field used for agriculture in North Tyneside.

Hand plough in Backworth village, depicting the farming heritage of the Tyneside region.

Marsden Rock and Grotto located in Marsden Bay, South Tyneside. Marsden Grotto is the only restaurant and bar in a cave to be found in Europe.

Opposite: *Grass on Little Haven Beach sand dunes, looking towards the South Groyne Lighthouse.*

The Millennium Bridge and the River Tyne, viewed at night from the Newcastle Upon Tyne Quayside.

Opposite: *The Sage Gateshead building, viewed at night from the Newcastle Upon Tyne Quayside.*

Carving on the reconstructed city wall near the quayside commemorating the ship building heyday of Newcastle Upon Tyne.

Opposite: *Late afternoon sun highlights the features of Wallsend Town Hall built in 1907.*

The historic building of the Tynemouth Volunteer Life Brigade Watch House, now a popular museum near the Tyneside coast.

Opposite: *The local landmark of the Spanish City, near the Whitley Bay seafront.*

A swimming and bathing pool cut into the rocky coastline of the North Sea in North Tyneside.

A sea wall built to defend the North Tyneside village of Cullercoats from the forces of the North Sea.

Ornate fountain in the grounds of the South Shields Town Hall, opened in 1910 and often used in Catherine Cookson television dramas.

The grand Georgian architecture of Leazes Terrace, serving as a hall of residence for city students.

Fields of rape growing in North Tyneside are a common sight due to the popularity of the rapeseed oil, which is extracted from the crop.

The well preserved Whitburn Windmill, situated in a residential estate in the South Tyneside village of Whitburn.

Tynemouth RNLI station located on the East Quayside at North Shields.

The HMCC Vigilant, an HM Customs offshore patrol vessel, heading towards the North Sea as it exits the mouth of the Tyne.

Statue of Stan Laurel, half of the world famous comedy double-act Laurel and Hardy, who lived in North Shields and attended the King's School in Tynemouth before becoming famous.

Opposite: Christ Church, the parish church of North Shields, was originally built in 1658 before being rebuilt in sandstone in 1792.

Saltwell Towers situated in Saltwell Park, a fine example of a Victorian park located in the borough of Gateshead.

Opposite: *Sycamore trees and the ruins of the Burradon Tower, a townhouse built around 1553 by Bertram Anderson.*

St Paul's Church near Jarrow. East wall stained glass window in the chancel depicting St Paul, the Risen Christ and the Venerable Bede.

Opposite: Bede's chair, an ancient oak seat between 800 to 1100 years presumed to have belonged to the Venerable Bede. Also in the Sanctuary, St Paul's Church.

The Rex Hotel and the golden sands of the Whitley Bay seafront.

Opposite: *Sunset behind the River Tyne and the Collingwood Cannons.*

Sandcastle-shaped shelters on the Whitley Bay sea front.

Opposite: *One of the 22 bronze statues forming the 'Conversation Piece' artwork located near Little Haven Beach.*

Abstract view of a wooden sea break located near the mouth of the River Tyne.

62

Dawn at the North Shields Fish Quay near the mouth of the River Tyne.

The North Sea crashes onto the sandy beach at South Shields.

Opposite: *Sunrise over the North Sea, looking south from above Marsden Bay towards Lizard Point.*

A statue celebrating a famous local South Shields' character, Dorothy 'Dolly' Peel.

Jarrow experienced some of the earliest Viking raids on mainland Britain when it was invaded in AD794. Although the invaders were defeated on this occasion, the inhabitants of Jarrow were not so lucky during later Viking raids.

The impressive Nine Arches Viaduct spanning the River Derwent in the Derwent Walk Country Park.

Autumnal colours in North Tyneside.

Newcastle United football strip immortalised as a sign for the Strawberry public house near St James's Park.

Opposite: St James's Park, home to Newcastle United FC. The cantilever roof pictured here is among one of the largest to be found in Europe.

Queen Victoria memorial statue located in St Nicholas Square, Newcastle Upon Tyne.

Opposite: *Statue of the 3rd Duke of Northumberland, in the grounds of the Master Mariners Homes.*

The Ouseburn running through a disappearing industrial landscape. The 800 metres long Byker Viaduct can be seen in the distance.

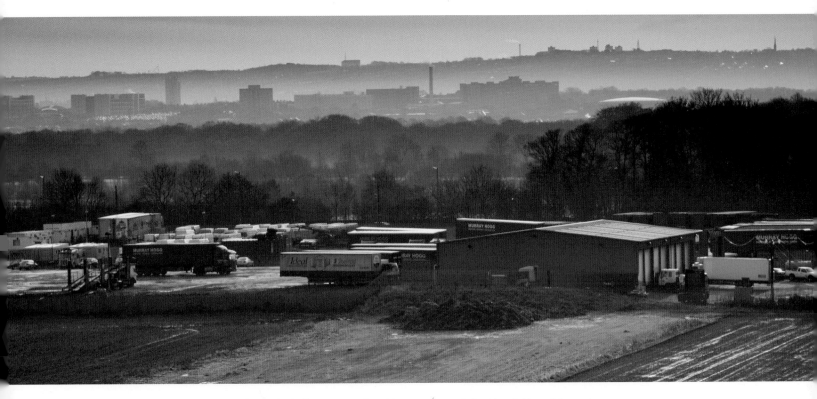

Mist rises from the hills surrounding Newcastle and the North Tyneside region.

*Sunrise over King Edward's Bay viewed from
near Sharpness Point. The remains of
Tynemouth Priory can be seen to the right.*

Rocky coastline and natural arch located on the south side of Cullercoats Bay found along the North Tyneside coast.

Lakeside reflections in the frozen water of Clockburn Lake in the Derwenthaugh Park.

The Ouseburn flowing through autumnal woodland in Jesmond Dene.

Architectural details of the Armstrong Building, part of the Newcastle University Campus. Completed in 1906, the two stone statues were included to represent science and the arts.

The modern façade of a Northumbria University campus, a complete contrast to the historic buildings of the Newcastle University.

The local North Tyneside landmark of the Cullercoats clock located in the listed Watch House building overlooking the bay.

The Earl of Zetland *was once a ferry working in the Sheltland Isles. Now it is a floating bar and restaurant moored in the Albert Edward Dock at the Royal Quays Marina in North Tyneside.*

Henry III added the great outer gateway known as the 'Black Gate' to the castle of Newcastle Upon Tyne during 1247 to 1250.

The Newcastle Castle keep was built by Henry II between 1168-1178 and is a fine example of a genuine Norman keep.

Newcastle Brown Ale has been brewed in Tyneside since 1927, with the recipe remaining unaltered since the start of the '30s. Traditionally brewed north of the river in the city of Newcastle, production switched to Gateshead in 2005.

The October of 1936 saw 200 people march from Jarrow to Westminster to protest against extreme poverty and unemployment in North East England. This march became known as the Jarrow Crusade due to the banners carried by the marchers.

Late afternoon light bathes the coastline of the North Tyneside coast near Whitley Bay, looking towards St Mary's Island and lighthouse.

Opposite: *Crashing North Sea waves engulf the rocky coastline of the Whitley Bay seafront.*

Electricity pylons distribute electricity across the River Tyne from Ryton to Newburn.

Opposite: *Ice-covered lake near to a residential estate in Killingworth.*

Tynemouth Front Street at dusk.

Opposite: The Grade I listed Theatre Royal photographed at night. Opened in February 1837, the Theatre Royal dominates the heart of Newcastle's Grainger Town.

The North Pier at the mouth of the River Tyne.

The setting sun illuminates the Collingwood Monument and cannons. Collingwood, who was born in Newcastle Upon Tyne, was an admiral in the Royal Navy and became famous for his involvement in several victories of the Napoleonic Wars.

Detail of Chinese artwork and design on the Chinese Arch heralding the entry into the China Town area of Newcastle.

Opposite: Bandstand in Exhibition Park, one of the numerous green spaces to be found near the city centre. The bandstand is the only remaining item from the 1887 Royal Jubilee Exhibition from which the park gained its name.

View from the mouth of the Tyne looking south towards Marsden and the Souter Lighthouse.

The South Groyne Lighthouse in South Shields, with the North Pier Lighthouse in the distance.

Excavated remains of the original foundations of the Roman Segedunum fort in Wallsend.

Opposite: *A space-age viewing platform overlooking the Segedunum fort.*

Above and opposite: *Sea buoys located near the mouth of the Tyne, in North Shields.*

The Column of Liberty reflected in a pool forming part of the eighteenth-century landscaped 'forest' garden of the Gibside Estate.

Opposite: *Looking through the stone pillars of the Gibside Chapel towards the half-mile, tree-lined walk heading to the Column of Liberty.*

Dawn looking over Sandhill and the varied skyline of Newcastle Upon Tyne.

Opposite: *The Cathedral Church of St Nicholas in Newcastle Upon Tyne was originally the fourth largest parish church to be found in England before becoming a cathedral on the 25th July 1882.*

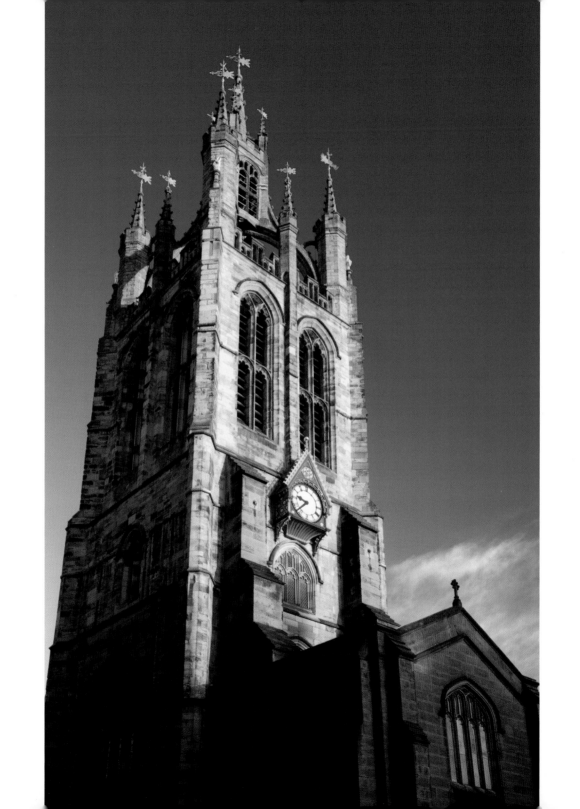

The rising sun spotlights the old mill in Windmill Field, located within the Cleadon Hills Local Nature Reserve.

Opposite: *Winter light gently bathes wild grass in an overgrown field in Sunniside.*

The chapel at Gibside was built in the 1760s as a mausoleum for coal magnate George Bowes.
The chapel, now owned by the National Trust, is still used for religious worship and wedding ceremonies.

Opposite: The St Thomas Church near the Haymarket of Newcastle Upon Tyne, was built in 1839 upon the site of
St Mary Magdalene, a former twelfth-century Leper Hospital.

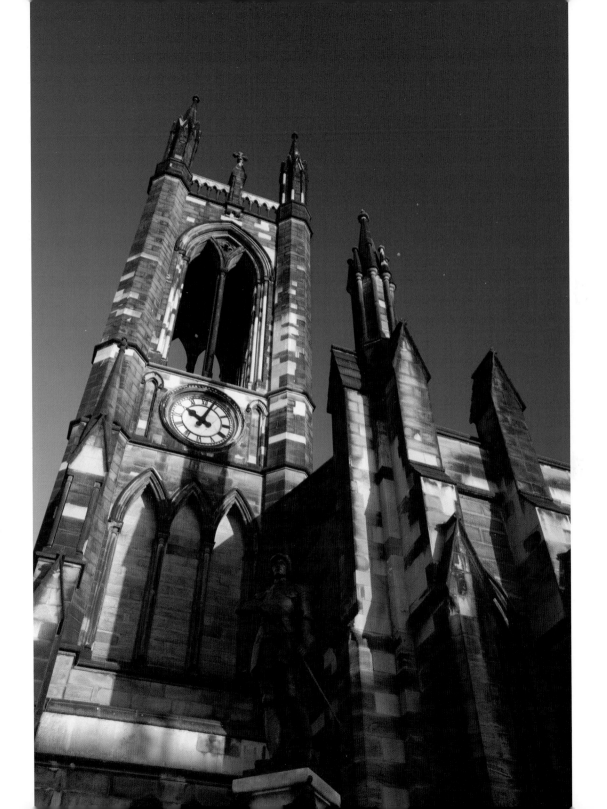

Alderman Sir Charles Hamond officially opened Tyneside's first park, Leazes Park in 1873. The lake pictured here was created along the line of the Lort Burn.

Opposite: Ferns in woodland sway in a light autumnal wind. This woodland is part of the Gosforth Park Nature Reserve, a private reserve managed by the Natural History Society of Northumbria.

111

The Swirle Pavilion located along the regenerated Newcastle Upon Tyne quayside.

Opposite: *Marina office on the River Tyne near the entrance to St Peter's Basin.*

Present day building structures reflected in the windows of an office block in Newcastle Upon Tyne.

Granite millstone from the Gallowgate Lead Works that were located within Newcastle City for over 150 years, finally closing in 1933.

Looking south on a mid-summer's day across the Tynemouth Long Sands towards the Priory, Castle and the mouth of the Tyne. Recently there has been a great deal of conservation work undertaken to help preserve the impressive dunes and vegetation overlooking the beach.

Souter Lighthouse, located on Lizard Point at Marsden, was the world's first electric lighthouse. It has been speculated that the lighthouse is also one of the most haunted buildings in the UK.

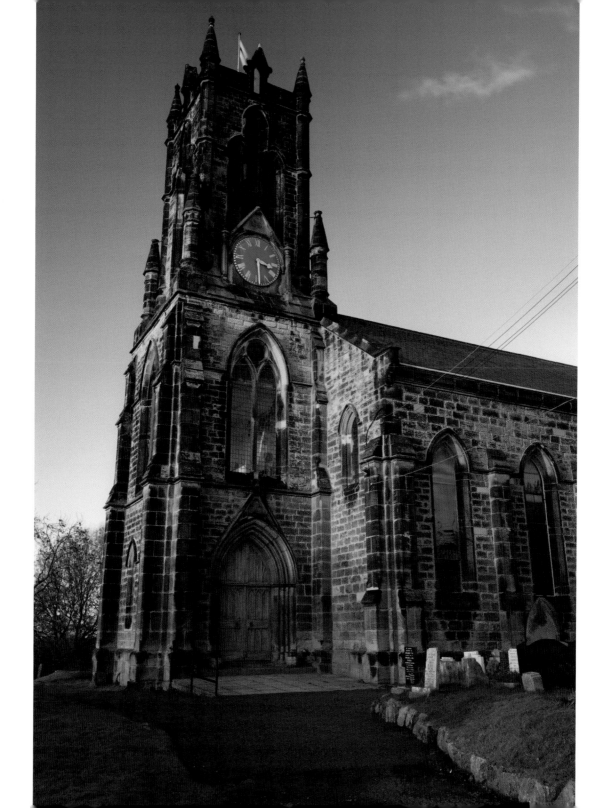

Early morning view of St Paul's Monastery in Jarrow with St Paul's Church in the distance.

Opposite: *Saint Alban's Church in Earsdon, a prominent landmark near the Northumberland border.*

The Grade I listed Parish Church of St George in Jesmond, is a fine example of Victorian art and architecture.

Opposite: The River Derwent running through Snipes Dene Wood.

Sunrise viewed from the north jetty in Cullercoats Bay.

Opposite: *The city wall of Newcastle Upon Tyne. The city continues to develop into an eclectic mix of historic and modern architecture.*

Agricultural land in South Tyneside looking towards the City of Gateshead.

Opposite: *The last rays of the setting sun paint a colourful scene across Killingworth Moor.*

Reconstruction of the main gate at the Arbeia Roman Fort in South Shields.

Opposite: *Rush hour traffic alongside Hadrian's Wall in East Denton. Hadrian's Wall was built to protect Roman Britain from raids by the Picts to the north, and stretched from the Solway Firth to Wallsend in North Tyneside.*

Marsden lime kilns, built from the late 1870s, were constructed to burn lime, which was then used on farms and in steel mills throughout the country and further afield.

Early morning light illuminates the crashing waves of the North Sea near Lizard Point.

Painting on a building in North Shields depicting characters from the history of North Shields.

Apartments on the North Shields Quayside.

Modern apartments continue to appear along the Tyne with the ongoing development of the region.

Opposite: *Sunset viewed from the Hebburn Riverside Park in South Tyneside, looking across the River Tyne towards the Offshore Technology Park in Walker.*

The history of the Tyneside Waggonways dates back to the seventeenth century when they were used to transport coal from the collieries to the Tyne.

Opposite: Sunset over the lake in Big Waters Country Park. The lake is a subsidence pond, formed by the collapse of old mine workings.

The Shield's Ferry offers a quick alternative for foot passengers trying to reach the other side of the Tyne.

Opposite: Rush hour traffic on the A1 heading south from Newcastle Upon Tyne.

Reflections of moored boats and surrounding buildings in the St Peter's Basin.

Looking from the Gateshead Millennium Bridge on the Newcastle Upon Tyne river quayside,
towards the Sage and the Tyne Bridge.

Frost-covered ferns photographed on a crisp autumn morning in North Tyneside.

Opposite: *Flowering Michaelmas Daisies photographed at sunset in the Rising Sun Country Park.*

Sunrise over Frenchman's Bay near South Shields.

Opposite: *The popular landmark of the St Mary's Island Lighthouse photographed in January against a natural backdrop of a pink sky at sunset.*

The iconic Angel of the North statue silhouetted against an atmospheric sky. The 'Angel', built on a former colliery pithead bath site, is one of the world's most viewed works of art with over 33 million viewers each year.